Lend a Hand

Poems about Giving

by John Frank

illustrations by London Ladd

LEE & LOW BOOKS INC. | NEW YORK

LEE & LOW BOOKS Inc., 95 Madison Avenue, New York, NY 10016

leeandlow.com

Book design by Kimi Weart

Book production by The Kids at Our House

The text is set in Centaur

The illustrations are rendered in acrylic, colored pencil, and pastel

Manufactured in Malaysia by Tien Wah Press, June 2014

10 9 8 7 6 5 4 3 2 1

First Edition

Library of Congress Cataloging-in-Publication Data

Frank, John.

[Poems. Selections]

Lend a Hand : Poems About Giving / by John Frank ; illustrations by London Ladd. — First Edition.

pages cm

Audience: Age: 6-10.

Summary: "A picture book collection of poems centered on spontaneous acts of kindness,

representing diverse voices and topical themes"— Provided by publisher.

ISBN 978-1-60060-970-1 (Hardcover : alk. paper)

1. Children's poetry, American. I. Ladd, London, ill. II. Title.

PS3556.R33425L46 2014

811'.54—dc23

2013032587

For Michael, Dick, Tia, and Gayle —J.F.
To those young and old who take time to lend a hand —L.L.

Sandwich

At noon, I noticed
the new kid
sitting alone
with only the words of a book
to feed her.
"Do you know,"
I was about to ask,
"if you tell the teacher
you forgot your lunch,
the cafeteria will give you one free?"
But instead I handed her
half of my sandwich,
and though I had
only half for myself,
after I ate it
I somehow felt full.

Puppy

The puppy we're raising
is the cutest I've ever seen—
cuddly and playful,
with floppy ears
and a wagging tail
and a look on his face that says,
"Please hold me and love me.
I want to be yours forever,"
and before long
we're going to give
him away.

He'll be someone's eyes
one day.

Jammin'

I made a new friend.
His name is Mr. Kellerman
but he says to call him "K-man,"
and he lives in a house
at the end of the block.
He just turned eighty,
and hasn't had any family
for a long time.
When I found out
K-man owns a ukulele,
I brought over the electric guitar
I'm learning to play,
and the two of us jammed
and traded riffs.
We're probably not good enough yet
to form a band,
but we didn't sound
too bad.

Hair

It took six years
to grow my hair this long.

A few quick snips
and most of it will be gone,
a ponytail
in the US Mail,
off to be part of a wavy wig
worn by someone
whose hair
sickness stole.

I don't suppose we'll ever meet,
but if we do,
maybe we'll look
like sisters.

Home Run

He was the klutziest kid in PE.

The way he'd shrink back

from the ball

and nearly fall over

with a hack at the air

made most of the class

nearly fall over

with laughter.

After class, I pulled him aside

and showed him how to square his stance,

how to hold his arms

and angle the bat,

and told him never ever

to take his eyes off the pitch.

The next time he came to the plate

he connected on the first swing—

and though the ball dribbled onto the field

no farther than a bunt,

my fist shot up

as if I'd just seen Davis or Cabrera

belt one out of the park

in game seven

of the World Series.

Stream

When our scout troop first got there,

I didn't want to go near that trash.

Someone else chucked it.

Not me.

So someone else needed to fish it out.

Not me.

As I stood on the bank

of that garbage dump of a creek,

staring down at that slime-covered can,

I almost felt sorry

for my gloves.

But I made my move

and picked up the can.

And then another.

And another.

And by the time all of us were through,

we'd uncovered a treasure:

a beautiful stream.

Song

The wallpaper's peeling,
the sofas are molting,
the air's thick with smells:
of old wool and mothballs,
and rubbed-on medicine . . .
of room spray and bleach
trying to hide what's not well.
For weeks our school choir
practiced this program,
these holiday tunes
we're about to perform,
yet most of the audience
stares at the floor
or out into space,
as if they don't even know
that we're here.
But when we start singing
I see, in the back,
a trembling hand lift
and tap out the beat
on a wheelchair's arm.

Trees

I doubt

many people

will pay much attention

to a few scrawny saplings

on this harsh city street.

But if any of these people

are here years from now,

enjoying the shade

in the heat of the summer

or the dazzle of color

on the branches in fall,

maybe they'll remember

what this street once looked like

and go to a place

in need of some trees,

and plant a few saplings

like I'm doing today.

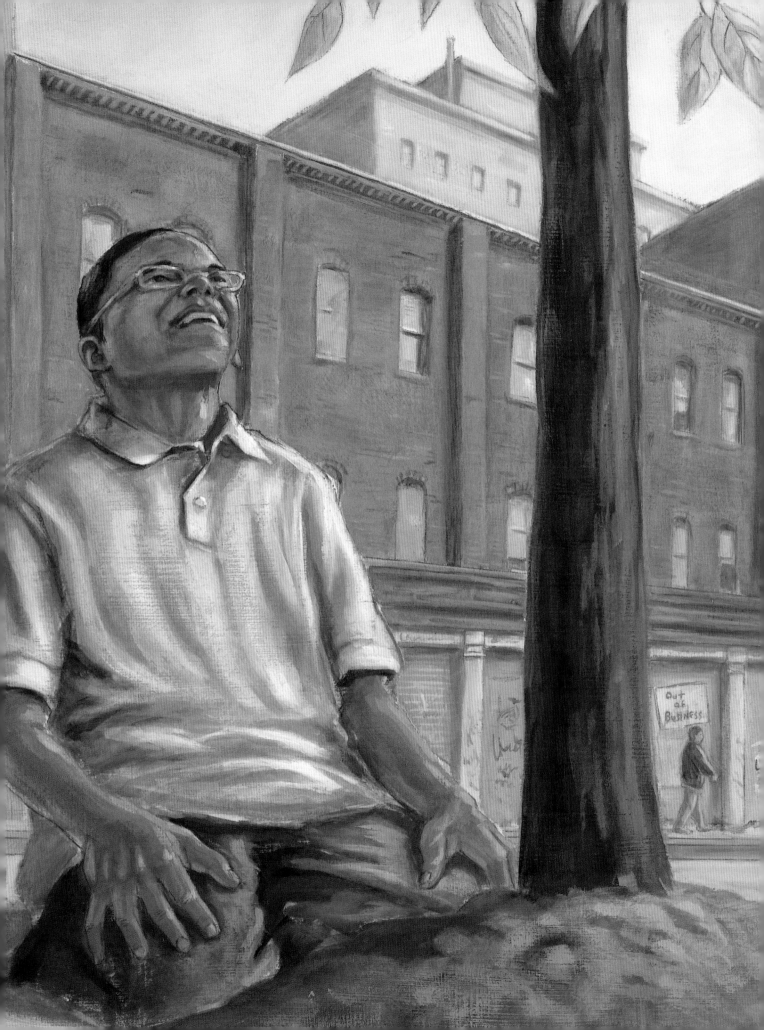

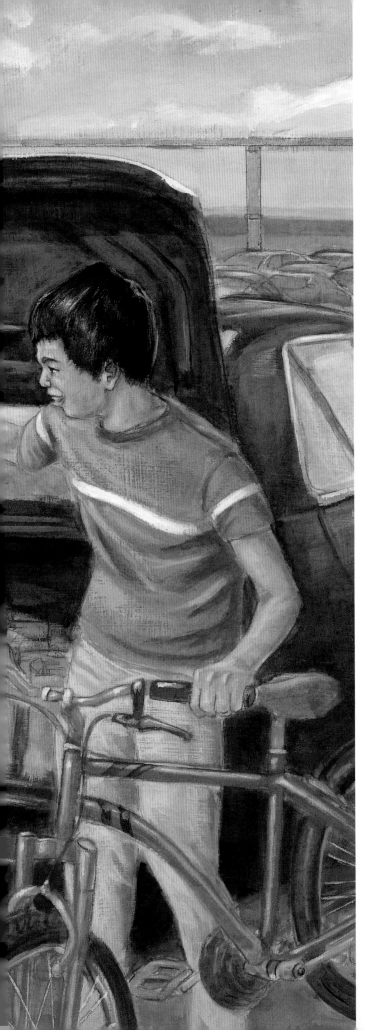

No Charge

The woman in the shop
inspected my bike,
spinning the wheels
and testing the chain,
then took out a tool,
did some quick work,
and told me my ride
was now as good as new.
I reached into my pocket
and pulled out my money,
but she waved me off—
"No charge," she said.

On my way home
I stopped by the grocery store,
but before I went in
I helped a woman load
bags into her car.
She reached into her purse
to give me a tip,
but I shook my head.

"No charge," I said.

Explorer

Saturday morning
I'm at the library,
trying to get an
ants-in-his-pants kid
to quit wiggling so much
so I can help him learn to read.
He tells me he'd rather
be at the park across the street,
rowing in that big toy boat
little kids all love to play in,
pretending he's an explorer
traveling all over the world.
He doesn't yet know
that on these shelves
are more worlds to explore
than he can ever imagine.
And I want to
hand him the oars.

Bus Ride

On a downtown bus,

had my earphones on,

filling my head

with some hard-beat sounds

as the streets sped by,

as the bus rolled on

till its next short stop,

where a man climbed on

with a rhythm of his own,

the rubber-tipped tap

of a walking cane,

but he couldn't step far,

couldn't make his way

through the jam-packed aisle,

so I caught his eye

and got to my feet,

motioned with a hand

toward the empty seat,

joined the standing crowd,

turned the music loud,

got back in the groove

with my earphones on,

swaying to the beat

as the bus rolled on.

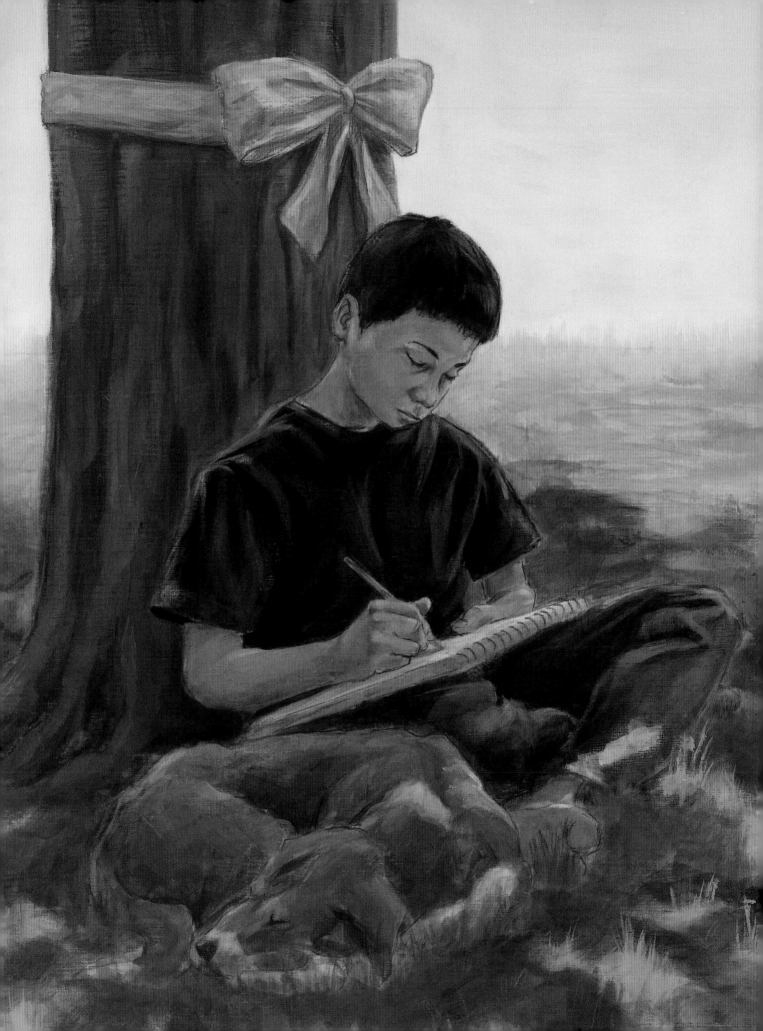

Letter

I know you don't know me...

Struggling to write neatly,
trying to decide what to add
or cross out,
I pause in my letter
to this person I've never met,
a soldier, thousands of miles away.

You must find it hard to be brave
when it's scary.
You must find it lonely
when you're far from home.
Do you sometimes wonder
what will happen tomorrow,
and if you'll be remembered
if you're not there?
You must want to matter.

I know you. ~~don't know me.~~

House

Pounding nails

is harder than it looks.

They don't always travel

in a smooth line.

They bend.

They twist.

And when you try to straighten them

or pry them loose,

they sometimes put up a fight.

When we're finished hammering

and this house is done,

a family will move in.

Hard times for them held on

like stubborn nails.

No Bounds

Multiplication

was always a chore,

till my grandmother

took me to her quilting club.

There I discovered

the simple marvel

of squares of cloth

sewn together by hand:

two squares by two squares

makes four,

three squares by three squares

makes nine,

the rhythm of a needle

making rhythms of shapes

to cover and comfort

a shivering child.

As I practiced my stitch,

I wondered aloud

if there should be a limit

to how far quilts reach.

Yes and no, my grandmother said.

A warm spread

should have a maximum size . . .

but the spread of warmth

should have no bounds.

◦ Illustrator's Note ◦

As I started the illustration process for *Lend a Hand*, I realized how important it was to capture the essence of the poems and the spirit of these young people doing selfless acts. I work from photographs and use ordinary people, not professional models, as references for the illustrations. The most surprising and rewarding part of working on this book was how people from all walks of life connected with the poems in their own ways. Here are a few of those special stories.

For "Explorer," the boy posing as the "ants-in-the-pants" kid had a hard time sitting still for the picture. His father was reading him a book, and after five minutes of restlessness the boy finally sat still to enjoy the story. The woman in the poem "Hair" shared how meaningful this poem was to her because her younger sister was fighting leukemia. For "Letter," the real boy was quiet and didn't talk much while I was taking his picture, but he finally opened up about his older brother, who is currently serving in the military overseas. On his cell phone he had pictures of his brother with his unit. The boys who posed for "Home Run" are actually brothers who play organized baseball. The older brother coached his young brother on the proper technique while I took pictures.

The amazing thing I came away with from this project is that when we step out of our comfort zone, take time to meet other people, talk to one another, and help those who may differ from ourselves, we find we have more in common than we think. I'll never forget all the people who trusted me and gave their time to lend me a hand.

— *London Ladd*